TSUNAMI Y

by Juliet S. Kono

TSUNAMI YEARS

by Juliet S. Kono

Bamboo Ridge Press

1995

This is a special double issue of *Bamboo Ridge, The Hawai'i Writers' Quarterly*, issue numbers 65 and 66.

ISBN 0-910043-35-3
Published by Bamboo Ridge Press
Copyright © 1995, Juliet S. Kono
All rights reserved.
Printed in the United States.
Cover Art/Divider Photos: A. Michele Turner
Book Design: Susanne Yuu
Author Photo: John Eddy
Typesetting: Wayne Kawamoto

NATIONAL
ENDOWMENT
FOR ❦ THE
ARTS

Bamboo Ridge Press is a non-profit, tax-exempt organization formed to foster the appreciation, understanding, and creation of literary, visual, audio-visual and performing arts by and about Hawaii's people. Your tax-deductible contributions are welcomed. Bamboo Ridge is supported in part by grants from the State Foundation on the Culture and the Arts (SFCA). The SFCA is funded by appropriations from the Hawai'i State Legislature and by grants from the National Endowment for the Arts, a federal agency. Bamboo Ridge Press is a member of the Council of Literary Magazines and Presses (CLMP).

Library of Congress Cataloging-in-Publication Data

Kono, Juliet S., 1943–
    Tsunami Years / by Juliet S. Kono
      p. cm.
    ISBN 0-910043-35-3   (paperback)
    1. Family—Hawaii—Poetry.   2. Natural Disasters—Hawaii—Poetry
    3. Tsunamis—Poetry.   I. Title.
    PS3561.0515T77 1995
    811'.54—dc20   95–10306
                                                                 CIP

Bamboo Ridge Press
P. O. Box 61781
Honolulu, Hawai'i 96839-1781
(808) 599-4823

10 9 8 7 6 5 4 3 2 1   95 96 97 98 99

Also by Juliet S. Kono

Hilo Rains, 1988

I have seen it over and over, the same sea, the same,
slightly, indifferently swinging above the stones,
icily free above the stones,
above the stones and then the world . . . .
If you tasted it, it would first taste bitter,
then briny, then surely burn your tongue.
It is like what we imagine knowledge to be:
dark, salt, clear, moving, utterly free,
drawn from the cold hard mouth
of the world, derived from the rocky breasts
forever, flowing and drawn, and since
our knowledge is historical, flowing, and flown.

—Elizabeth Bishop

Contents

PART I
The Elizabeth Poems

For Elizabeth May Boydston Lee

Rain
and
Red
Roses

"Mother, Mother," you sang,
"Mother pin a rose on me."
Convinced she was the prettiest rose alive
in a dress with its shower of baby roses,
a cloud of white crinoline,
teardrop pearls,
and the enormous, red rose,
a burst heart,
radiating across one breast,
you watched from the landing
as she and Papa came flying
down the staircase at Ahualani.
They left with the houseguests.
Leafy kisses blew
around you at the gate.
Forever, you thought. Yes, forever.

One day, she said, "So long! Good bye!"
and slipped around the corner grocery
only to forget who
or where she was
as she spun a shower of petals

in an unraveling of thorn and leaves
among the oranges,
apples and nectarines,
and flew into her past.

How love has taken a new turning.
It's no longer Mother,
but Elizabeth the child who now hangs
her eyes on you,
grips your hand,
rubs the skin of your elbow between her fingers
as if it were a nickel.
Elizabeth, whose frail body you cup
to catch the soft fall
of what she has to say on the way to the car.

We take her for a ride.
It starts to drizzle.
Chattering away,
the light wind of her voice
patters like the rain on the window.
So this is it, I think to myself,
life in its last reduction:
the seed, cracked and open,
its heart left to dry.

Love
Letters

Many months have passed
since the diagnosis,
and you're still grieving for her.
She's not dead yet.
But she's lost, like a child is lost—
her mind the ocean floor,
where she kicks up sand
and churns in the water.

Al, we call it, or AD—
never by its real name
as if mentioning the *word* would bring bad luck—
the need to cross one's self across the heart,
throw back to the ocean half of one's catch,
turn three times and pray to the East.

Papa's and her letters,
written during their courtship,
are tied with a faded, red ribbon
and sunk in a safe deposit box at Bishop Trust.
Long ago, she gave them to you
for safekeeping. At the time

she exacted a promise from you,
that you would not read them
until she was dead.
We twist down the spiral staircase
curled like a strand of seaweed
into the cold room of vaults,
the heavy thud of door distinct as your sadness
following us everywhere. There,
you turn over the bundle of letters
in your hand like unbelievable money.
"I'm so tempted to read them," you say.

You want her back,
the feisty and independent one,
the one who could, at eighty,
do ten knee bends in aerobics class,
dance a smooth jitterbug
and shuttle like the tide
to and from the house about her business.
Not this Elizabeth you mourn,
the one who can no longer reason,
who points and giggles at fat people
and smells, sometimes, like the ocean.
Time slides like Dali's clock.
Elizabeth is surprised
that she once was married and had a husband,
that she once gave birth to sons.

Symmetry

After a discussion of Blake's "fearful symmetry."

By the time we were married,
we were much older.
We wanted to have children
but as my mother said,
we were too "highly colored,"
like momiji leaves
along the banks of the Awajima
in late October.

As if knowing we wouldn't be having children,
your mother gave us this gift,
this last flow of experience,
an exercise in futility,
one hour baths,
looking the other way
when she drops food
or dirties her panties.

You're fitting her
into diapers at night,
slipping on her house slippers,
helping her to swallow the stone pills
by moving the slow river of her throat.

The clock on the wall
has turned on its heels,
and the other shoe fits,
the shiny Mary Janes that stomped up the porch
and slammed shut the front door
of her childhood home
where she is, once more,
pounding on the candy-striped walls
of an upstairs bedroom
on Indiana Avenue, Vallejo, California.

Suspicious

Elizabeth reserves all her grateful looks for you.
In the morning she extends her arms like a child's,
when you get her up,
and gives you a wink when you pour her juice
or butter her five-grain bread.
"She's so sweet . . .
doesn't she give you those *same* looks?"
Hah! You must be joking.
Elizabeth thinks I'm hired help,
the Japanese maid
whose hands are small,
the proper size.
To her, this is the only
good thing about me.
It means I can lay shelf paper well
or get into the corners—to wipe.
And most of the time she's wary.
She watches whatever I give her to drink,
questions the pills I give her,
if I'm putting the appropriate
foot in the right pant leg.
She thinks I'm going to run

off with her silverware,
her tortoise comb, her shower cap, her jewelry,
her beloved son.
She keeps her eyes on me, all right.
As if to say: "You can't fool me!"

Two
Queens

Elizabeth and I have what you call
"a women's thing."
No kitchen can have two cooks.
No beehive, two queens.

"Huh? What is it you said?" Elizabeth asks,
listening in on our every conversation.
Nothing is sacred—busybody be.
"Honestly, mother, I'm getting you an ear horn.
Besides, I'm not talking to you," you say
to dampen her wings.

Watching TV, she sits next to you.
She cuddles your arm, fondles your ear.
You pull her touchy hands away.
Should I come to plant a kiss on you,
Elizabeth shoots a sharp eye at me.

She doesn't like it, too,
when I'm the one to feed and bathe her.
"Where is he? Where did he go?"
Only you! She wants only you.

"He's mine!" I'm told in no uncertain terms.

One day, she thought you'd been killed
on the way home, perhaps, in an accident.
Another time, Saddam Hussein held you hostage.
"Darn guy!" she cursed the dictator.
"Don't worry, Mother," I reassured her.
"See my face? I'm not worried."
"Hunh, you'll never be."
And it's all hugs and kisses
when you walk through the door.
"Oh honey," she drips and oozes,
pouring it on,
advancing with her arms outstretched.

Some days Elizabeth tattles on me.
She calls you at the office and complains
that the dishes are still in the sink,
the tea bag on the drain board,
the flowers not watered.
"The nerve," I say, "your Mother's got nerve.
Who in the world does she think
combs her hair, cuts her hangnails,
tweezes the hairs on her chin?"
"It's something you have to work out.
I'm not there, remember?
Besides, she doesn't mean it in her heart."
Doesn't mean it in her heart?
What woman doesn't, I think to myself
of this venom;
calculated, its tongue long as history.

"I'm trying to understand!"

We have our moments, this old woman and I.
But Elizabeth is dying,
sucked in on herself like lips over gum.
And some days are better than others,
now that I've found
she's much more pleasant
when she gets off on the right foot,
has a good breakfast,
a good morning constitution.
I rub her legs, feed her royal jelly,
wheel Elizabeth out in the sun.
Learn about myself and love.

Old
Biddies

In our building we have a lot of old biddies,
frail, with canes and walkers.
We meet them, occasionally,
in the elevators or hallways.
And your mother,
even in her dementia,
still likes to show them up.
She throws back her shoulders,
stands a little taller,
inflates herself like a puffer fish,
then sails through them
like the *Queen Mary*,
leaving them bobbing in her wake.

Champing
at the Bit

We champ at the bit.
We're hot to trot
at the starter's gate,
Elizabeth and I in the mornings
as we jockey for position.
Sometimes, she pulls ahead—
"mix my Metamucil,
pass me the toilet paper,
pour my mouthwash."
Control and lucidity,
moments she can command it.
Sometimes, it's me out front,
leaning into the neck of the wind,
the mane of it flowing into foolishness.
Here we are, two women
reduced to such childishness
and almost always just for the sake of it.
It's pitiful
how we're at each other's throats,
how we want to show each other up,
the way we lap ice cream in front of each other,
read the newspaper slowly when we know the other wants it

or savor the last morsel of chocolate pie.
It's "nah na nah na boo boo" time,
unexclaimed but felt,
the tongue stuck out,
the hand with the candy behind the back, to tease.
This is the way we drive—
neck to neck,
shoulder to shoulder,
either ahead by a neck's or body's length
or falling behind into the pack.
This is the way we get through the quarter-mile,
the half, the mile,
the day, the night, the week.
But it's the long haul that counts,
isn't it?
The long striding of care,
the heart's length,
winner's circle and wreath.

Recognition

Some days, Elizabeth doesn't know me.
At the day care center, she has to be coaxed like an old brood
        mare
to the car parked at the end of the Futura Stone walkway.
Like a horse in a trailer, she hugs and flanks the door.
Driving out, I look over and decide
a treat would do us both good
and turn into the neighborhood shopping center.

Ice cream, and Elizabeth still doesn't know who I am.
We sit in the car and eat quietly.
Then trusting that I won't hurt her, she lets me
drive her up the hill to where we live,
overlooking the city. On the way she notices landmarks:
the graveyard at the top of Wilder,
the old stonewall,
building numbers marked at the entrances.
She lets out a whinny of recognition and claps her hands.
"You know where we are—who I am?" I ask.
"Of course I do, silly."

"Whoa, Bill," she says, when I jerk to a stop in our parking stall.

I lead her into the building and up the elevator.
Her smile broadens with each floor we pass.
Five. Six. She calls out the lighted buttons.
Ninth floor. She steps out, looks down the hall toward our door,
and swinging her rump, she quickens her pace
like an old horse headed for the barn.

What
to Be

All morning Elizabeth cuts flowers, pretty thoughts—
spring bouquets—and carries them down the hall
to place on my table. There's a low pall
hovering the city; the vog's high, caught
without wind. And too, the smell of salt, wrought
iron, weighs our throats. Time has such gall,
irritates her eyes. Afternoon: a short
nap. (Termite weather. Expect an onslaught
of insects tonight.) She wakes up. Distraught
with heat, she takes herself to scalding like
burnt cream. I gaze out the shutters—a strike
of light on the gardens. My eyes deceive me?
Things don't know what to be: fish or lily
pad; flower or butterfly; bird or bee.

Shower

In her illness
Elizabeth believes we do this deliberately,
the washing of her body.
She blames me,
her Japanese daughter-in-law
for having made keeping her clean a fetish.
Angry, she says we do this to torment
her soul, the shower a hot
spray of needles we subject
on her moon-colored skin.
She hates it even more
if *I'm* there to wash her.
She wants her son,
the person she thinks of these days
as her lover, or husband, or father.
Memory and privacy,
she cries at their loss
as I soap her down like an old car.
What protestations!
And as I listen to her,
I think of these bodies
we have given so freely to men,

yet feel ashamed of
when in the eyes of another woman.
How she fawns
when she thinks a man's around.
Today, she bangs the walls.
"I hate you! The water's too wet!"
Hanging onto the safety bars,
she pitches back and forth
like a child,
wanting to be let out at the gate.
I wash her back.
She spins around
in my soap-lathered hands,
and loosening her face in mine,
she glares.
She sticks out her tongue,
and biting down on it, she squeals,
jowls swinging, arms jiggling.
Then, in a dive of both hands
between her legs,
she drops to a semi-squat, simian posture
and thrusts her pelvis bones forward
like mountains in an antediluvian upheaval.
In a gesture of obscenity,
she unfolds her petals
and displays her withered sex to me—
the same way boys moon, flip the bird
or grab their crotch and waggle their tongues—
the profane she feels but can't articulate.

Knowing

After bathing, I want a Coke. I'm so
thirsty. You apologize. You forgot,
you say, to buy some, the kind I like; but
will go out for the six-pack, Classic. "No,
never mind," I say to push the guilt. Slow
clouds and rain outside. No moon. I shut
the bedroom door between us, lie down, knot
us in sulks, but not before I catch low
said words: "childish . . . menopause." Name-caller,
I don't contend. *Know* you care. Darling, we're
six years older, that long in marriage tied,
and yet, you still surprise me. Earlier,
in a twilit room, I watched you bathe your
aged mother tenderly as a child.

The
Scolding

Sometimes, I must be bigger
than what my heart desires,
or what others make me out to be

when I wait for you
to wipe your mother's mouth,
wrinkled as a dried fig,

or wash her hands, sinewy and curled,
that cling like wet leaves
on your arm in steadfast dependency.

Husband turned caregiver.
Forced into the tender clutch,
son and mother,

because she can no longer wipe her nose,
cut her toenails or wash herself.
So tell me, what's worse—dying or not dying?

I try to assist in this barter
between the young and old—

this give and take of helpless looks.

You don't resent it; she's your mother.
I'm the daughter-in-law,
often blind-sided by the fist

of her words in my outsidedness.
Your mother! Evenings, she whines
like winds that blow across the Pacific.

She paces her room. She cries and carries on.
To console her, you pat and stroke
her back broken by a thrown clock

and children who rarely come to visit.
I hide. I disappear into our bedroom.
I wait, hoping for five minutes.

But you don't appear.
When I go out to find you,
your mother is draped on your shoulder

like an old shirt.
Look how she mocks me!
Animals around a fire,

we circle, territorial,
rinsing the scent of ourselves
on the sofa, the chairs, the curtains.

Doctors would insist
she is incapable of this.

But what if—what if

some of the last things to be forgotten
are the wiles of a woman?
Irritated and angry,

that you look like, like *lovers*,
I go after you
with a mother's guava switch and tongue.

Elegant

Lucinda King calls your father the most
elegant man she's ever met. You're just
as elegant, I tease. "It is your lust
that makes me feel so," you fire back. Toast
I'm eating gets caught as I laugh. "I would
be elegant, perhaps, but first I need
to be fitted in a Savile Row tweed,"
you say. "You, on the other hand, should
not fear, my soignée Juliet." *Soignée.*
(No one's called me that before.) If movie
stars, we'd be ripping off our clothes at this
moment like a crumb trail! Not now honey
your eyes say. "Hey, take it easy," you hiss,
"Mother's still awake and watching us kiss."

Morning

The middle of the night and Elizabeth's
awake again. She thinks it's morning. Lock
tumblers roll as she opens and closes
the door for the newspaper. A far clock
chimes. You roll out of bed and steer her back
to her room, only to find her gown's wet.
Diaper change made, lights snap off to a matte
darkness. To steel your patience, a kiss set
on her cheek. "Love you Mom," I hear you call.
Back in bed. "I feel like Job," you say, chilled.
"I half expect someone to tell me all
my goats and lambs and asses have been killed."

Missing
Person
All Points
Bulletin

Central to all units: be on the lookout for an elderly Caucasian woman last seen in the area of Prospect and Magazine Streets. She was wearing a red, white and blue blouse, red pants, white walking shoes and a multicolored jacket. She is 85 years old. She wears glasses. She walks with a slight stoop. She thinks she can fly. About 5' tall, she has gray hair and answers to the name of Elizabeth, or Betts, or Mama. Shout "Hey!" or "Yo!" and she'll turn around. Party may be walking in circles. Party may be walking, looking at the sky. She may be talking to a leaf or tree, a bird or dog. Approach with kindness. Otherwise, she may scream and shatter; otherwise, she may think she's died and gone to heaven; otherwise, she may call you "Papa," take your face in her hands and kiss you. If seen, detain and notify her son, or Central, or God. KRO two four three, Missing Person APB, 2:45.

Feeling
Smug

They give it to you all the time
at the drop of the hat.
People full of advice.
If you let them,
they would tell you how to wear your hair;
get through the terrible twos; deal with teenagers;
get rid of fleas, birds in the air vents, thrips.
Now it's advice on how to care for your mother.
They're expert
because they always know
of someone like her,
in the same condition,
who almost burned the house down,
walked out and was found wandering on the highway
or arrested for shoplifting.
Or indecent exposure.
So, it's "Put up a black cloth by the door."
"Turn the broom upside down."
"Never whistle in the dark."
"Never leave an open umbrella in the house."
This, and on and on.
Oh, they're full of it.

At the end of the day,
when we're folded down
like summer lawn chairs and tables,
the watermelon seeds she drops
are slimed off the floor,
iced tea glasses are dried and stored,
and she's finally in bed,
all sweetness and reason,
we feel smug,
sheets tight up to our chins,
the night light like halos above our heads,
knowing things are easier said than done,
knowing tonight, to make her sleep,
her ice cream was laced with Valium.

Caring
for
Mother

No greater love has a son, you say, than when he has to
  watch Lawrence Welk or Mr. Rogers with his
    mother;
  overlook the mustard she drops
on the front of her blouse while eating a hotdog;
  wipe her because she no longer remembers what a
    vagina is;
  fetch her a glass of Metamucil in orange juice to
    keep her regular;
  change her diaper in the middle of the night;
  floss and brush her teeth, or don't floss
and brush her teeth because she keeps on swallowing
the toothpaste, and be embarrassed, later,
when someone says she must have
soiled her pants because she smells funny,
but he can't say anything in front of *her*—
to explain that it's just bad breath;
  help her swallow her pills by placing them at the
    back of her throat;
  put on her shower cap and tuck in the curls under
    her direction;
  wait for her in a last minute "tinkle" and be late for

work;
        take her to respite care, find she doesn't want
to stay there, only to have to bring her home, again,
and forget about the much-needed vacation—
and to console himself, buy a good book;
        sweep up after her meals;
        not scold her because she's unlearning everything;
        kiss her on the cheek even if her wrinkles smell
            funny;
        sing old songs with her to stimulate her memory,
reminding her of his father—her husband—her parents, her
            cats,
how old she is, her name, her birthday, her children,
his name, his wife's name, her grandchildren;
        turn away and look to the past to remember her as
            she was,
and not as she is, to remind himself;
        calm her down when she has a temper tantrum
at the airport turnstile and must be budged through like an
            old horse;
        never show the grief he feels because he has lost a
            part of her;
        turn on the VCR and watch musicals
featuring Hermione Gingold, Fred Astaire and Cyd
            Charrise,
or cartoons and *The Little Rascals*—action holds her attention;
        rinse out soiled pajamas at two in the morning;
        dress her when she strips off her clothes at the
            hairdresser's;
        pat her on the back until she stops crying
because she doesn't understand why
she can't possibly go out unless someone's with her;

        put on her pink house slippers as he kneels
on the floor while she sits on the bed forwarding the wrong foot;
        read Robert Frost at 3 a.m. in her day/night reversals
and she can't sleep;
        place a fork in her hand when she eats with her fingers;
        watch her apply a crooked line of lipstick and say she's
            done it well;
        watch her primp, dust her nose, plump her hair
like a young girl in front of the mirror, only to wonder
if she sees anything, and if she does, to wonder what;
        decide he can no longer take care of his mother.

After the
Jupiter Symphony
Conducted by
Pinchas Zukerman

It's the eve of war.
Once home,
we have hot chocolate with your mother
who sits in pink slippers,
feet high above the floor
and tucked under the chair like a bird,
taking wing. She's shrunken.
It's as if all the air
had been let out of her arms and legs,
her face, throat and chin.
But her head is clear tonight.
A dowager, old as Methuselah,
and borne into peace by age,
she doesn't like what she sees on TV.
"Give the land back to Mesopotamia,"
she says.
"Give it back to Sumeria, Addak.
Better yet, give it back to the gods."

Last
Concert

These days, we tap our hands and feet
to the themes and variations of someone old.
Your mother, stricken with dementia,
drives up and down the scales of her sanity,
her off-key, birdlike solfeggios.

Mornings, you put on swim trunks
to go into the shower with her,
to wash the jarring note of her body.
I help by guiding her hands on the bath rails.

We're in this together.
Not long ago, we made a conscious decision
to take care of her at home—
at least we'd give it a try we said—
the same way couples make such decisions

to have or not have children or pets or a musical instrument
like a piano in the house.
We know each day brings with it a different composition,
something discordant and alarming:

a wrongly buttoned blouse, a crooked line of lipstick,
a face rouged like a clown's.

This was a good mother.
Someone who meant no harm,
who, for years, took care of your sick father,
her parents, children and the stray animals brought home.
There was always someone or something to take care of.
And this is her last concert,
one for which there is no standing ovation,
no calls for an encore.

Bearer
of
Water

You cradle your mother's head
on the soft side of your arm
and slowly lower her into water,
clear, warm, amnion.
She raises, then
drops her arms,
hands dripping like oars,
the water lapping
the cool sides of the porcelain
and her body.
Woman, your child.
Bearer of water,
you bring the soothing offerings
and homage of a good son:
salves, a bar of simple soap,
salts and oils, unguent herbs.
You take a washcloth,
soak it with water
and draw it over her forehead
as if in a baptism, to anoint her,
before you wash
the rest of her body.

She follows your face.
She never leaves it,
even as you soap
her most delicate parts,
the body she gives up to you,
privacy she relinquishes
in this room, warm and still,
above the gentle sounds of water,
the cooing noises of approval she makes.
How long these days?
Some of your saddest
when you gaze at her,
the mother you grieve for,
the one dying without you.
Young. That she was, once.
There, as in the photograph
on the traveler's chest,
ducking the wind-laced spray,
a day at the beach with your father;
you, the only person she knows now,
the one who ferries her across water.

Bedtime

You have your mother sit
the side of the bed she sleeps on.
Gently, you push her
into a lying position.
She has forgotten how to do this,
the same way she has forgotten how
to get out of bed in the mornings.
"Very good, Elizabeth."
"Thank you, Daddy," she replies,
her legs still dangling the side.
You lift their dead weight,
heavy as carcass,
and slide them under the covers.
You take off her glasses.
You then ask if she would help
in saying her prayers:
"Now I lay me down to sleep,
I pray the Lord my soul to keep.
God bless America.
God bless Elizabeth."
This is all she remembers. This is all she can say.
Just as she drops off to sleep,

you take the white rabbit from her arms
and place it beside her pillow.
"Good night, Mother."
You lean over, kiss and pull
away from the black taste of her mouth.
You must miss your mother.
Not this woman who sleeps before you
whose breath smells primal,
animal and vegetable,
this woman who comes between us.
Later, I hear you drop into your chair,
your spirits sinking,
the field of dark flowers you walk in,
the snapping of stalks.
And I know that not a night passes,
in all your sadness,
when you have not given yourself the luxury
of this one thought—
that for her sake and ours,
she dies before she wakes.

Elizabeth's Prayer

Our Father,
who art in Cleveland,
hallowed be Thy game.
Thy Kingdom come,
Thy will be done,
on Thursday
as it is in Heaven.
Give us this day
our daily bread,
and forgive us our trespasses—*yes!*
as we forgive those who trespass against us—*yes!*
Lead us not into temptation,
but deliver us from weevils
for Thine is the diner
and the power
and the glory
forever and ever.
Omen.

The Lights
in the House
of Her Mind

Every light in her house stood ablaze.
The music of Sibelius floated out
along with the *chink* of fine china
and silverware, the high ring of Austrian crystal
in a house full of books, a collection of duck stamps,
her needlepoint and travel memorabilia.
The children came out and played in the light that stretched
itself in ladyfingers across the lawn. The lovers lost
       themselves
in the shadows of the trees, and the grandparents
rocked on the porch swing. She sang unabashedly.
Life was good to her. The old were first to leave.
Her parents. His. Then the children,
called away by their lives: friends, cities and wives.
And as if someone were gradually turning off all
the lights in her house,
one by one,
until only one light burned dimly . . .
the house becoming quiet, dark and still.

PART II
Tsunami Years

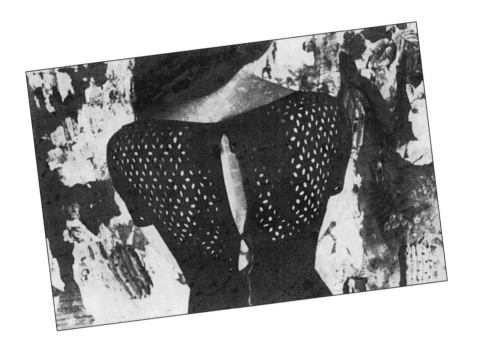

For my Aunty Dot who saved my life

Name

Only after the guests held up their cups
and shouted "Banzai!"
the year before the War
when we were at the same wedding
did the reception settle
into talk and rounds of whiskey,
you say in the story
of how you met my father.
You also tell me
about the half-drunk men
who sank into bravery and leapt
the stage of the social hall
under the Buddhist temple
to sing ribald street songs,
which made the women blush.
Closing your eyes, you mimic
how men slapped their thighs,
swayed their bodies
and shook their heads into the beat
like angry fists.

My father noticed you
while you watched the singers.

I imagine it's the same way
I've seen you clap your hands
and swing your head side to side,
almost prettily,
in time to the music
that made him send you a drink
and into this lifetime.
You drifted your eyes
across the room.
You saw him braced innocently
against one of the pillars
as he gave a wild wave of his hand
that changed your lives.
You acknowledged his drink,
lifted your cup in a toast.
A tilt of your head, a sip.

You had just come back from California.
Five years of picking apples
on Uncle Shigeru's farm,
baskets slung on turned-up hips.
During the winters, you worked
for a rich white family
who ate rice with melted butter,
whose bodies smelled too sweet,
cream and sugar.
I missed the rains, you say,
the waves that dashed the rocks of Hāmākua
and cracked the shell of water into a fine mist.

"Nobody knew
how I was forced home by your grandmother.

I had fallen in love
with a man whom she believed was kotonk.
But he fooled everyone. He became a doctor.
He even gave me an English name.
Nellie. Nellie. That's what he called me.
Even your father calls me by that name.

And his name,
the one in California?

Jack. His name was *Jack.*"

Atsuko's Wedding Day

Today, I'm a bride.
Today, I give up
the promises I made long ago—
of marrying for love,
of never picking up after a man,
of never scrubbing his back.
The grooming woman
comes to shave my eyebrows and face
to make me more beautiful.
She powders the smooth nape
of my neck curved for a man's pleasure.
Ricelike talc is showered
into the plunge of my neckline,
and my lips acquire the deep bloom of red flowers.
Hair that swings like a pendulum
takes all morning to comb into a wide, black fan
for the ancient ceremony,
while a thick hot wind blows in
through cracks in the house
and the chickens scuff the earth
in the dirt-dry yard.
No one can keep

the dust off the tansu
and out of their nostrils
and the food safe.

I wear a mon coat and black kimono;
my husband-to-be, a black borrowed suit.
Together, we wash our hands—
in a basin outside the plantation town's
tiny, green temple down the lane—
for safe passage through life's gateways.
Before the altar
we clap our hands in prayer
and hold them high in the air.
We rejoice and chase all evil—
for lives that stretch, endlessly,
like the sea from the islands.
We praise the gods.
We praise the splendid
pearls of rice from the fields,
matsu from the mountains,
squid from the ocean.
For blessings and happiness.
The priest waves
a paper wand over our bowed heads.

We hold a small party
under my husband's
best man's house down the gulch,
hidden by banana trees
where mosquitos nest in water-trap stumps.
Magenta and yellow,
the colors of the kimono I change into,

the road of the evening.
These are my offerings.
They show how well I walk
on the hard-packed dirt floor
among the guests; how well
I serve them hot rice wine.
A way I enhance my negligible dowry.

We spend our honeymoon
in my parents' plantation home.
The room has no curtains,
no ceiling. Our clothes are hung on nails.
The first time is love without sound.
He moves quietly
into me, like the sea,
the altar of my hair taken down,
the long strands spread like seaweed,
as the rest of the house
sinks in sleep and falls
below the waterline
of a stray cough, a child's cry,
a dog's fitful bark.
We cannot sleep.
Our naked bodies, wakeful in promise,
rise in the moonlight
above the tall cane that moves in currents
and splashes against the house.
From pillowing arms
there is no low talk of death or tragedy,
of crying without reason,
the disappointment to come
when all our sons die.

Outside, an 'ōma'o stirs in the shadows.
Touches the glow of our young faces.

Going
Somewhere

He feels his life going somewhere.
He buys a small house in Shinmachi,
bides his time like fish circling bait
and dreams to the rhythm
of the old Waiākea clock
that he may, someday,
be able to buy a house
where Japanese are forbidden to purchase.
So there, by the sea,
in little dockets of time,
in small increments
of early contentment,
the skin of his wife darkens.
Sand coils around her ankles
and she enjoys her food.
It's the salt air, she says,
as she fills out her dresses.
Soon there is one child,
then another.

And we surround him
whenever he brings home his catch,

his one arm wrapped around her,
his robust wife,
the other making wide sweeps
of encouragement for us to touch the fish—
his young daughters
who cling like barnacles,
who clap and "ooh,"
amazed at his sport and luck.

He brings home bucketsful—
sea cucumbers, octopus and shellfish—
for the family to eat.
There's a war on.
He saves on food
in time of black markets
and the rationing of gasoline and tires.
"To do my part.
To give brain food to the children,"
he says as he throws back
his head in laughter,
his gold teeth
a run
of fish in moonlight.

School Boy
from Up Mauka

(21 students and teachers at Laupahoehoe School were killed in the tsunami of 1946.)

You ran outdoors
to look at the receding sea.
Open and bare,
it was as if the tale
of the Five Chinese Brothers
had come true, the story
your teacher had read to you.
Somewhere,
on the other side of the ocean,
the first Chinese brother
had drunk all the water.
And here, on this peninsula,
how everything glittered:
red stars, black sea urchins, pink anemones.
With pants rolled high,
shirt tucked in at the waist,
you walked into shallow water
and picked up the red, gold and silver fish:
pāpio, weke, āweoweo.
Fish for a good boy to take home.
Fish for supper.
"Look, look," you yelled to everyone,
pointing at your prizes.

A sudden roar.
As in the story,
the first Chinese brother
who could no longer hold the water,
let it rush out
and into our side of the world.
If I could, I'd have stretched my legs into stilts
like the third Chinese brother
and plucked you from the sea.
You dropped the colors from your hands.
You moved up to face the wave.
And in your wonder, all you could do
was gape and point at
what curled,
magnificently, above you.

Whirlpool

for Dorothy Kawashima

Water comes up
to the level of your mouth.
It laps your lips and nose
like small harmonic tremors—
the Earth passing through you.
Water neither washes in
nor recedes now,
everything below surface
except your head.
Below,
your body reaches up like a flower stem
or a length of chain that supports a buoy marker.
Feet tangled in rubble,
body held fast as an anchor,
you're trapped. You can't move.

The child you carried is gone.
A red shred of her jacket
you drag in your fist
is the only thing left.
You bring it to your mouth
the way animals eat their children

to save them.
On your side a torn purse
dangles like a broken arm,
and somewhere around you,
a hundred silver coins
have slunk and swirled
and cut light
on their way to the bottom.
Money from a dance fundraiser.

Soon water pulls out.
It grows in concentric circles.
Bodies, houses, trees and animals
bob up, roll over
and whorl in the drain of the bay.
Moored at its edge,
you watch everything in orbit
fall in.

Tori's
Tale

The waves high as tree crowns.
And I am an old woman,
a frayed rope slack with age,
body tangled in a loose, morning kimono,
feet in wobbly wooden clogs from the old country,
and bad legs,
swollen and waterlogged like driftwood.
When a wave rumbles in,
my daughter-in-law tries to save me.
I peel her bird grip from my bony arms
and wave her and the children away.
"Go!" I yell above the roar.
"You young ones—save yourselves!"

The first wave smashes the house.
It picks me up like wind does a yard bird.
It churns me around and over
the neighbors' houses, lanes, fences
and people's screams.
Dragged out toward the ocean,
I grab the beard of shore grass,
my body and hair
being pulled seaward like kelp.

A young man swims me inland.
He places me into the limbs of a tree
and coaxes me to perch like an old bird,
when another wave pounds us without mercy.
No older than my youngest son could have been,
this boy is tossed in the surf
like a hat, a cane tassel, a stick in the flume.
He sinks like shoes.
I unwind my arms.
A twisted rope, I throw my body
for his outstretched hands.
Bodies and foam swill past me
between the grove of trees.

My son finds me before evening.
I am still hugging the tree.
I sit, naked from the force of waves,
and exposed
are what my son has never seen
since their firmness in his childhood:
my breasts—
sagging, flat and blue,
nipples stone purple—
like broken shutters on an empty house
in winds rising.

Joji
and
the
Iceman

I'm just there, watching
people bring in the bodies
from the ocean,
the line of them growing
like so many Buddhas
in the front of Dodo's Mortuary.
So many bodies to prepare.
The iceman taps me on the shoulder,
and walking away, he yells
at me to watch the truck, the cab he pops into,
as he backs toward the bodies
sprawled on the army surplus
cots and stretchers.

He sloshes about in rubber hip boots,
black apron pants, leather gloves
and blows blossoms of cigar smoke
in front of his frozen face
as if to kill the smells.
He gives everyone orders.
Like blocks of ice
or marbled beef slabs,

he swings the bodies up,
and I'm told to slide them
deep into the bed of the truck—
the bodies to be stored
in the town icehouse.

Bopping his horn,
he comes for me in the morning.
He takes me to the icehouse.
On the vaulted doors,
someone has placed a bouquet of flowers,
which he whips off as he grunts
and swings the doors open.
Overnight, the bodies have frozen together.
I circle the blocks.
I top them off with the flowers he had thrown aside
and peer into the ice of eyes and faces.
I take the pick he hands me.
I chip the ice away;
sometimes pierce flesh:
an arm, a face.

Sea Flower

Long after the sun flares on the horizon.
Long after Bunemon pulls the tarpaulin
like a blanket over the drying lauhala
and locks the chirring chickens in the henhouse,
circles it in ripples,
to check for loose wire
a mongoose could sneak under,
take a hen down
and disappear into the tall cane.
Long after Shige gathers the sun-stiff laundry,
the winds pick up speed,
chill the land-warmed air
and rattle the loose house boards.
Long after the stars slide
behind the loom of night clouds,
the full and fish-eyed geckos
tsk tsk like unhappy mothers,
fluid mice drain into narrow cracks
at the sound of our feet,
approaching the kitchen
where the dog is chased from under the table,
and with my grandparents, we gather

on long benches to drink
green tea, crack roasted chestnuts,
eat baked sweet potatoes
and chat.

Shimmering below a boiling kettle,
a blue kerosene light.
From an old filament bulb
that hangs in the middle of the room,
an orange glow floats out
and bathes our faces in a warm wash.
I place my sleepy head on Mother's shoulder.
Pulling away her kimono sleeves,
Grandmother pours tea into fisted porcelain cups.
Our eyes widen in this dim light.
They narrow, again, in the steam of tea
when the cups are brought to our parting lips.
Mother says from out of this blue and orange air,
"We were lucky, weren't we, Daddy?"
And my father nods his head
like a sea flower,
as he blows a long wind
above his blue teacup
as if across a vast sea.

Coral
Chips

No trace of us,
the family who lived there.
No trace of the red house,
the one with white curtains,
high children's voices,
shuttling in and out on the sea breeze,
the father who teased
he caught Hawai'i
on a "whitewash" day of fishing,
the mother who hummed
"Begin the Beguine" to the kitchen sink,
the black sedan in the garage,
spare tire on its trunk like an old lady's bun.

No. Nothing of the house
with its front porch overlooking
the white coral-chip walkway
that connected to steps
with a cat furled like a rag rug
you had to skip over
to get to the doorway.

We have come back to this place
after the disaster.
We look for something of our lives.
I walk around, pick, then drop,
pieces of cut glass, a headless doll,
a cracked teapot.

I run up to a twisted car.
Not ours! I cry into my arm
dashed across the hood.
And I can't find my father.
Has he disappeared, again,
into the waves? Then I see him,
leaning on the only tree
that has survived being uprooted.
He walks over, puts a hand on my shoulder
and I want to cry.

I don't look in his eyes.
I look down my bandaged legs
to my delicate feet in a sister's oversized shoes.
I kick up a few coral chips,
blow off the grass, the salt,
and place them into my borrowed dress pocket—
scattered stars of life to keep.

Water
Spots

My mother's eyes hold the distance.
She doesn't look into the camera.
Her eyes are clear, her mouth relaxed,
and she is dressed in a new, rayon,
white flower-printed dress,
the flowers huge as magnolias.
Her hair is upswept into a wave,
a month before she is to lose
everything to the sea.

She wants this picture taken
to show off her daughters.
We sit on a bench,
my sister sporting a neat boy cut,
me balanced on Mother's knee.
Mother's legs are crossed at the ankles
with a detail of white shoes
like whitecaps at sea.
My sister and I have toy planes in our hands.
The cameraman,
Mother says years later,
jumped up and down
but could not make us smile.

My mother found this picture
in the water,
near the foundations,
what was left of the house.
The only signs of tragedy, now,
are the water spots
along the edges
and on the side of Mother's face,
spreading
the way fire burns across film.

The Peddler

Mountains rose above
our village like hands in prayer.

She shuffled from house to house
in a wide hat and straw slippers
and sold her fruits and vegetables.
Beneath the scallions, tangerines
and fingers of bananas,
she tucked a Bible.
After exclaiming how
sweet her fruits were,
she began preaching.
She called Mother pagan
for worshipping the Buddha.
"New country, new religion," she said
to Mother who stroked us,
her salt-sticky children,
while shifting her feet,
one over the other,
gritty with black sand
that blew in from the beach.
Mother was polite,
open to different views.

In the tsunami disaster,
the vegetable peddler's husband
was found feet first, his body
stuck in the mud like a stick;
and her daughter, barely weaned,
was caught on some tree.
The villagers plucked her off
like sweet summer fruit.

Some people, my mother says,
found Christ that day;
others, left Him.

Lost
Birds

All morning,
Mother prepares
for the pull of lead on a fish line.
Hooked in the stomach
as when fish swallow bait,
she moves in a frenzy.
She sweeps, mops, dusts,
places magazines in piles,
edge on edge,
stacks dishes according to size,
plumps pillows and shakes out the rugs.
A hasty lunch
ends her tidying.
She drags me into the bedroom
for an afternoon nap.
To prevent my falling off the bed,
she builds a wall—
piles of futon in a breakwater around me—
and lays out
water-salvaged books and toys.
She is sighing heavily by this time.
She drops into bed beside me

and begins to cry.
She dozes in an expanding silence.
I lean over and place my cheek
against her tear-splattered flush.
"Nice Mommy," I say, stroking her face
in the hot air
that banks the afternoon stillness.
Drifting endlessly,
the house creaks
and rocks like a small sailboat
in some windless sea,
and we are two lost birds
who find refuge on its listing mast.

Atsuko's Dream

Sleep is the fear my body falls into.
Sleep is my head being pushed
down into water by a dead man's hand.

Sleep means seeing
the swirl of their hair,
my children being swept out of my arms.

I hear them cry out and swallow water,
small arms flailing and rising in the air
before they are pulled under.

Sleep is finding them dead again,
open eyes gray and fixed,
blank in their love for me.

Eyes magnified, made multiple,
tiny white bodies and faces beneath
the surface in sea-grass movements.

Small round faces come and go,
like coins, just beyond reach.

What
My Mother
Confided
in a Moment
of Sadness

We were alone the first time since the disaster.
You children could finally sleep through the night
so I had no excuse
to avoid your father.
I spent hours by the window.
There, my body felt soft,
and I belonged to myself again.
As the moon rose, I watched the beams
reach out for the white flowers,
the thinning trees
and the ocean.
On a night stand beside me,
with one hand,
I spun the bone-china figurines
that were scattered on a mirror:
a dog, a horse, a ballerina.
With my other hand, I supported my face.
Soon, I detached myself
from the light, the flowers, the figurines,
and turned into the room—
water to forbear—
to where your father lay and waited eagerly,

unbuckled at the waist
and stretched across the bed
in an old undershirt,
one arm lifting his torso on an elbow.
He looked hard into my face.
Pulling my arms into wings,
I unbuttoned my dress.
He wanted to help,
but I let fly a hand when he touched me
and caught him at his wrist.
Lifting my dress, I let it
drift and splash on the floor.
Then I turned to him and the window.
I looked far off and saw,
once again, the flowers, the line of trees,
the curve of moonlight on water,
smooth and harmless,
as I clutched my slip to my chest
and dragged the smell of the ocean to bed with me.

When Atsuko Came Up for Air

I excuse myself too often,
to bathe,
to sink into water.
Private immersions I call them.
Satisfying and personal,
the passing of body through body.
And yet,
it's not as if
I don't want him
to breathe eagerly on my eyes anymore.
It's not as if
I don't want him
to press my shoulders, lightly,
into the comforters.

All of him
I don't really mind.
How can I explain
that he is simply not like water?
His body neither fluid
nor copious
in molding around my body.

His stroking never measures
up to the strong pulls,
the surges that force
resistance and resignation
before its will.
No, there's nothing quite like it—
the pull under
to the bottom of the ocean,
the rainbow colors of my breath,
rising and moving away from me,
that places me closer
than anything else in life
to that awful thrill of death.

Atsuko
Between
Stars
and
Waves

It's been three years since the disaster,
and I'm still trying.
I get up in the mornings
and feel as if I'd swum
great distances between the stars and waves,
the night making no delineation.

Every morning I feel seasick.
Nausea wells in my body
in waves and dry heaves.
I retch over a square white basin
and run water
over the yellow trace of bile.

Like everything I couldn't save,
I cannot save these children,
blue and amphibian,
who come swimming
between my legs.
Tagged and laid out,
they hold no cry.

Another boy.
I go home with my arms empty.
The other women at the hospital
look at me as if I were a freak.
Swollen and lumpy,
my breasts make little ponds
on the front of my dress
as I sit at the window,
overlooking the bay
in a body taken to the edge,
and I ponder the clean cut,
the body's revolt
of little boys
caught between the sky and the sea.

Stop

A wave looms in the background.
It is higher than the telephone wires
and moves up Waiānuenue Avenue.
Looking over half-sloped shoulders,
men run with all their might,
lurching their lunch pails behind them,
dragging jackets,
others with morning papers rolled in their hands.
One man with a painter's cap pumps his arms
as if drawing water from a well.
Those farther behind him
will be caught by the wave.

In our family album,
for years and years,
I've looked at these running faces.
Half-moons of disbelief in smiles
carved deep in their faces
like bad scars.
Don't they know
that they've already been saved
by time and age?

I'm tired of surprises and death.
I want to tell them:
"Take deep breaths. Clasp the pain in your sides.
Stop! Stop this running, forever!"

No-Place Children

Some people are mountain people,
says my mother.
See? You can tell.
Look. Their bodies sway in the sun like trees,
the whites of their eyes hang like clouds
on the dark mountain of their eyes.
See, too, how their feet, root crops,
pull them into the ground.
And their hands and arms,
rough and hard, feel like bark,
the shafts of their hair singing in the wind.
They always look up—have you noticed?
afraid of droughts and hail.

Some people are sea people like your father.
Their bodies are slick,
slicing through water like wrasse fish.
They're not afraid of water; they smell of salt.
And it begins with their feet,
the scaling. As they grow older,
it happens on their elbows,
to the backs of their hands and knees.

Their hands, too,
begin to cup like clam shells
around small fish and stars trapped in tide pools.
When they cry, dry salt
whitens in patches around their eyes.

When I used to go down to the sea,
she says, the sea knew
that I was different somehow.
The waves started to swell.
They swept further inland to rope my feet,
and the winds picked up speed.
Offshore breakers
raced in with comet tails.
As for you, my no-place children,
I drowned five times to get you.

Womanhood

When I was three,
a tsunami hit town.
"Daddy, Daddy, save me,
don't let me drown."
He saved me
and my common-type dolls.

When I was sixteen,
another tsunami hit town.
I cried to my daddy,
"Daddy, Daddy, please save me,
don't let me drown!"
But he let go of my hand!

I still dance
to what broke on my life.

Hāla'i Hill
—1957

Tsunami sirens sound
a steady wailing tone.

My sister and I rise from the breakfast table,
leave the steaming cups of tea
and quarter-moons of Saloon Pilot crackers
half-eaten on the table.

Mother makes a ritual of preparedness.
She turns off the stove
and glides like a ship into the bedroom.
She packs. In a White Owl cigar box,
she places the family valuables:
> our genealogy
> juzu beads
> mortuary tablets
> Grandfather's hair and nail parings
> bank books
> human ashes in an envelope from Japan.

She drives up Hāla'i Hill
from where we watch the bay
and its green churned water.

Around us, car exhausts hiss, collectively,
from lines of cars,
coming from other low-lying areas.
We tune in on someone else's radio
as we keep an eye on the ocean.
Low and sultry,
Rosemary Clooney sings
between static broadcast intervals.

I think of our house while we wait.
Dust coiling in the morning light,
our starched school dresses,
Mother's food-stained uniform on a bamboo rod,
a prom lei drying on the wall,
crepe-paper roses on my desk.
Will they be spared,
these treasures in our rented house,
the X on our coastal inundation map?

My sister and I rest with our backs to the car.
We stare down the willful sea
with eyes that float,
while Mother holds onto her box
of valuables tighter than a child.
But Mother is anxious to get back home,
to start the night's dinner.
And we want to be on our way to school
where boys lean out of the windows
and shout to us from their roadsters.
We wait and wait
for the triple blast,
the all clear.

PART III
Painter

For my son, Eric Rikio Kono
1967–1994

For my father, Yoshinori Asayama
1911–1994

Day
of
Death

Grandfather watches koi rise—their lips pursed
kisses—in his sunlit reflection. Once,
pining for Japan, he built and planted
a garden: temple grass, bonsai, ponds. Since
then, he's found the garden no longer grand.
Only the fish mesmerizing, their fins
a thousand fans. A gentle fish, I blend
into his vision. "Sore wa Zen," he says.
Later, he cleans the ponds. "All-u time too much-i
egg." With bamboo, he hauls waterlilies
out and dries them along the banks. Eggs clutch
like seed pearls on roots, hanging like beards. He kills
to save a few; no aesthetic of harm.
A day of death can be this way: sunny, warm.

Only
Son

Bunemon Oshita 1889–1954

1.

The eyes of the villagers were like stones
in your pockets that held you
down to filial piety in the Otagawa.
But your drunkard father staggered
once too often, like the river,
into the house. You wanted
nothing to do with him.
You wanted nothing to do
with your warlike country
or the mother and sister you couldn't save.
You sailed off with a willow trunk,
took your books, ointments and carpenter tools,
wore wooden clogs on your feet,
and in your hand, twirled a straw hat
fringed with your imagination—
the woman in a photograph not yet taken
and children full of promise
like the persimmon seeds
you carried in your pocket.

2.

A bulb flashed into her eyes.

Her solemn face was mailed
to you as her hand in marriage.
On a ridgeline
you built a house on stilts
for rain water and rats to run under.
Nearby, you planted a line of persimmon trees.
On the slopes the caneland
you burned and cleared
soon delivered its sweet harvests.
And the children appeared,
in such abundance,
all six of them. One day
you were on the dock, arriving.
The next, you were a grandfather
seven times over with more coming.
I was the only one you took
for rides on your broad immigrant shoulders.

3.
The summer you died,
the persimmons lay where they fell.
You were not there to gather them with me.
Flowers in the garden grew wild,
the grass, tall, and above the fence line.
Like your cancer it was growth no one could stop,
growth that spread like cane fire.
And as if they knew,
the dogs howled,
fish swam in rapid circles.
I ran and ran across your fields.

4.
Years later, a cousin of mine tells me
how lucky I was
to have ridden your shoulders,
to have sat on the porch at night,
listening to you play your fue,
watching you smoke your pipe.
She feels she's missed something:
a new tune, a shooting star, a boat on the horizon.
Am I as lucky as she thinks I am,
to have felt such love?
Unconditional—
an open field of flowers,
water filled to the brim of the catchment—
when so young,
that even now
the roundness of grief follows me,
the full moon lush as a persimmon.

Penmanship

1.

My father had the most beautiful signature.

Driven by compulsion,
he made fast little circles in the air
above the paper with his pencil,
the lead he wet with his tongue.
The motion had the same spin
as the red wind on the cane roads
that picked off hats
and bent the grass seaward.
When his pencil finally touched the paper,
his hand spooled toward the edge
in the force of its own momentum.
They were like waves, curling,
or pipelines.
No. More like coils of wire,
the spirals, the neat ellipses,
he drew between the lines of his notebook
like an architect.
Penmanship.
That's what he practiced he said,
reliving the round-face boy

slouched over the desk
at the old Ōlaʻa plantation school.

2.
A cold wind from the mountains.
Inside, a tea kettle boiled over,
and Mother had rice cake, frying.
I was learning how to write.
After watching me over my shoulders,
my father placed me on his lap—
the only time ever—
held his hand over mine
and guided it across the paper.
Haywire. That's how tangled
my writing became when he let my hand go.
"Chicken scratch," he called the scrawls.
I didn't care. I learned, quickly,
that if I lost control on purpose,
he would take up my hand,
again and again.

3.
Paralyzed, my father
tosses sounds in the back of his throat like a bird
at the sight of my handwriting.
He scratched the air
the time I signed under the unsteady X
of his living will,
the revocable living trust
and durable power of attorney.
Once, as garage manager,

he did it with such flair,
his name authorizing service done on a car.
"Thanks, Asa," the patrons called out.

"Help me to die easy," his eyes say.
And I do want to free
him of the pain of his last spin.
But he pulls in like a sea anemone
whenever I touch him.
"It's chicken scratch, Dad," I say.
"Here, give me your hand."

A
Spin
Around
Town

I pummel my father's back like a taiko.
Although he winces when struck,
he signals me to continue pounding
with a lift of his hand.
Pushing his thoughts elsewhere,
he gazes out the window and watches
birds lurch a stoic path upwind.
He can no longer speak.
His frail bones are bird hollow
in the sureness of my hands.
After the '46 tsunami,
he never talked about
being trapped in the car,
taken out to sea and lost.
Long ago, when I asked him what it felt like,
he could only shake his head,
the possibility of his death, unspeakable,
the silences sinking
into thoughts of water swirling around him.

After later tsunami
he'd take me for a spin around town

under skies
like the gray undersides
of birds' wings
to look at the power and destruction of the ocean.
We used to stop,
get out of the car
and survey damage done
to the stands of banyans and ironwoods,
the houses and businesses
strung along the beachfront.
At the sight of everything,
he was lost for words.
Once, he took me to the Hukilau Hotel
to see the wave heights
of the '57 and '60 waves
that overflowed the hotel lobby—
heights marked on the picture window
with red and blue fluorescent tapes
for tourist information.
When I was still young,
he said that if I kept eating like a bird
I would never grow taller
than the 1957 marker—
a wave height of five feet.
But look at me. I've outgrown him
and the height of waves he fears.

Today, I circle the town with him.
I drive along the bay front,
hoping he will break through his silent water.
I then drive toward 5 Mile,
believing he wants to look out at the ocean,

to watch the tides run out.
He motions to stop
the car across the Carlsmith Estate
near the old mullet pond.
He lifts his head.
With his mouth shaped like their hootings,
he points to the pintails and plovers
that rise, circle, and bear north.

Late
Praise

Japanese fathers give praise
thin as toothpicks, limp as saimin noodles, rough as bone meal.
My father couldn't say anything nice.
He'd rather jump off Honoli'i Pali.
Just not his style. His style? Attack the head.
He called me "stupid," "dumb," "bakatare."
And best to do this in front of people,
to make shame,
break the proud daughter bone
that straightened the back
and hauled in the immovable
will of the mouth. And it's the mouth,
after all, he just had to get to—
like mud wasps on the housewalls
in summer.
It was too smart for its own good,
that ugly sphinctered mouth.
It got his goat, cut his bait and hurled its turd
like no Japanese girl's should.
He knuckled the head,
connected to the angry face
and the O ring of the mouth

that was ready to snap—
mean with the teeth of disappointment.
There was always the taste of something bitter,
like melons and medicine,
year after year.
Now, my father's old.
He cups his ears to hear,
pees with bad aim and walks with a cane.
In his wallet he keeps
a yellowed newspaper clipping of me.
Wrapped in Saran Wrap,
it looks like an old Shinto talisman.
He shows it to his friends.
"Das my daughta," he says,
rapping the picture with a knuckle.

My
Mother's
Sugar
Loaves

My mother grows pineapples in her backyard.
What started with one plant
increased to several rows of them.
She uprooted the wing-bean vines,
Swiss chard and cherry tomatoes
to cultivate this spiny fruit.

The island she lives on
has always been noted for sugar cane.
Her father once owned acres.
In her town
anyone will tell you that it's impossible
to grow pineapples,
the climate too wet,
the fruits needing a lot of sun.
But her pineapples thrive.
Sugar loaves, she calls them.

The neighbor children
call her the "pineapple lay-day."
Friends come with sacks of papaya
or bananas to exchange.

I've heard her apologize to friends
that it's too bad they only grow in summertime.
She wishes she had more to give,
generous that she is.
"If I had more land . . . ."
Good omiyage for friends.
Mezurashī off-island gift.

Out back and showing me her crop,
she says that people on the Big Island
had been growing the wrong thing all along.
"They should have grown pineapples."
And she sticks a new crown into the ground,
for emphasis.
She taps a fruit,
selects one for us to taste.
"This year too rainy. Might be sour."
Back in the house, she slices the pine
and pops small wedges into her mouth.

She passes a plateful of pine for me to try.
She's afraid it's too acidic.
I can't tell. I only know it's a bit
tart, but sweet.
And it's like taking a bite
into a slice of my childhood.
Some other fruit before me,
another kitchen table
where she and my grandfather
discussed an ailing cane crop,
the seamless edge
between poverty and paying the bills.

At night, she goes out to chase the cats
and takes a last walk in her garden.
She bends over to pull
a stray weed or two,
then straightens her back
to survey her plot of land.
Queen of the hill,
she sleeps under the smell of pine fruit
and the rustle of long, spiked leaves.
I hear her behind our doors,
this woman whose breath
rises and falls like the backyard wind,
who, at her old age,
still dreams of plantations.

Tongue

Dust flew into my eye.
My mother took my face
into her hands like a melon,
came at me with her tongue
and placed her lips around my eye.
It looked as if she were sucking
out my eyeball,
the way she sucks out fish eyes to eat.
She swirled her tongue
and cleansed my eye of its irritant.

Honeycomb of lungs
sticky with infection
held me to the sick bed for days.
She placed her mouth over my nose
and sucked the green muck
as if she were slurping noodles.
Her tongue helped clear
my blocked nasal passages,
and heaved my wheezing out like bath water.

After a walk in the canefields,
a bee in the ear
had me spinning like a top.
I banged into the wash buckets, gate, clothesline,
zigzagged like a drunk
or someone blind.
Mother grasped my hands
and secured me between her legs,
and came down on my ear with her tongue.
She slid the tip in and left it there.
Without a flinch,
she retracted her tongue
with the bee curled on its tip.

My lips on your lips,
my lips holding your tongue,
a learned truth.

Caregiver

Father tugs on his leash all day. Tires her.
Although he doesn't speak well anymore,
he can still say "no" like a tough old cur-
mudgeon: "You're cra-a-a-a-zy!" coming from a store
of expletives. Thus said, he refuses his
insulin shots till *he* is ready. Drinks
pills when *he* wants to. Will not shave. Piss
scrawls down his pant legs and wets his socks. He stinks,
but if she insists he change, he'll not. "How
you take this," I console mom, caregiver.
"He's an old dog, isn't he?" She shrugs, her
lips tight. But now I see, she no longer kow-
tows to him, growls over a newfound bone:
"You listen! Or else I'll toss you in a nursing home."

Typical

My father is dead now,
and my mother goes to the hairdresser's
once a week.
"Funny man, he was," she says.
"Didn't want me to have my hair done all the time."
When I ask her why, she doesn't know
if he was just plain manini, a piker,
or if he didn't want her to look pretty.
"What for? Why you want to curl your hay-a?"
he complained.
All the time jabba, jabba,
morning to night, she says,
and makes duck-bill motions with her hands.

My poor father.
My mother never shed a tear!
And we can only remember
him as a grumbler,
a real Taishō.
But she tells me,
he was just a typical Japanese man—
nice to outside people,
grouchy to the family.

Nowadays, my mother,
who is irrepressible,
pats my father's urn and talks to him
in a one-sided,
lone-mynah-on-a-wire conversation.
"Daddy, I going church now."
"Daddy, I going painting class.
I'll bring home some sushi for you, okay?
You be good."
But she concedes,
it's no fun this way, really.
"Cannot fight with him anymore!"

Before
Time

They said to marry only Japanese,
and only *some* of our own kind;
not zuzuben, batten, kotonk,
hibakusha, eta, Uchinanchu—
night-soil carrier, big-rope people.
Before time, they said not to marry
keto, gaijin, haole—hair people, foreigner, white;
saila boy, Chinee, club foot, one thumb, chimba, mahu, glass
      eye,
harelip, bolinki, pigeon-toe, Pologee, Uncle Joe's friend,
      Kanaka, cane cutter, mandolin player, night diver,
      Puerto Rican, tree climber, nose picker, Filipino,
      thief, bartender, jintan sucker, Korean, paniolo,
      farmer, bearded,
mustachioed, Teruko's brother, daikon leg, cane hauler, left-
      handed, right-handed, smartaleck, Christian, poor
      speller, commie, Indian, leper, Hakka, cripple,
      drunk, flat nose, old, Jew Pake, chicken fighter,
pig hunter, moke, ice cruncher, opium
smoker, one-side-eyebrow raiser, fat,
olopop, skinny, Punti, thick lip,
albino, kurombo.

A Scolding from My Father

To R.H., D.K., M.M.

What kind Japanee you?
Nothing more worse in this world
than one Japanee
who like be something
he not.
No matter how much you like—
no can!
No can *be* haole.
Who the girl? You know, the Michael girl.
The doctor's daughta, good-looking,
live in the big house Wailuku Drive.
Big eyes, nice car, blonde hair.
You like talk like one haole?
You like big eyes?
You try live their house.
No can *be* Chinee.
Rich. Wong-family-rich.
Daughta go Honolulu, dorm at Punahou.
We no more their kind money.
Me? I only one mechanic.
Your mother, Baker II
at Waiākea Waena Elementary School Cafeteria.

And no can *be* Hawaiian.
Like Keliʻi family daughta.
You know which one—the smart one.
Good hula dancer, fast swimmer, going mainland.
You like dance like her?
Nice nose too she get—some tall.
You like one nose like her?
You dreaming, girl.
Come from her mother side.
You one flat-nose Japanee
because your mother get flat nose.
So why you like ack different for?
Why you like be something you not?
You no more shame or what?
Eh, you no figa too,
that maybe these guys
they no *like* you
suck around them?

Old-Time Friend
Talking Any Kine
at One Party

Eh, you know what?
Japanee, we ratha eat than have sex.
How you figa? Look.
Look how we make the food.
All this fancy stuffs. Everything nice-nice.
Take a look at this. Ridiculous!
Fancy kind net from one daikon.
Flower from one radish,
flower from one cucumber
for put mus-ted on top.
Very cleva but so much work.
And uka pile food:
plenny noodles,
musubi, sushi, salad.
Eh, what this—fish eggs?
Uh huh, whale meat. Eh, this illegal eh?
And all kind sauces too—
miso, shoyu—and mus-teds
in fancy kine dish. Must be
you went take out your fancy
dishes today,
bamboo pattern Noritake, eh?

All this to give power.
We even give the food names
by how we grab um, roll um, color um.
And worse of all, the *smells*.
You notice we like eat stink stuff:
baccalau, bago'ong, natto, daikon, kōko, ham ha—
but no worse than the kine smell,
if you know what I mean.
Two things smell like fish,
and one of um is fish.

Eh, we feed them till they ma-ke you know,
the men. They get real fat.
After they eat,
they so full, no can do nothing.
And the wahine, they so tired,
they drag around like *snails*.
But they stay skinny, live long time.
Eh man, no get me wrong.
Not as if the wahine no do nothing.
After all, get uka pile of us.
Let me tell you something, tho',
they neva really *enjoy* the stuff.

You ever seen cats mate?
The female so bored,
she blinking her eyes.
She like get um over with so she can walk
away, go back inside the kitchen.
Better for eat; more good, more *satisfying*.
Same difference with Japanee wahine—

no can be bothered.
You try watch the birds and fish.
Only the males—they get 'cited,
all nerjous—shake all over.
But watch, only at the start.
In the end they like hurry up, too,
so they can go back—where?
For eat of course.

You know something?
I get one real ke-ke face. You notice?
And bad scars from watcha may call it—
impetigo. See my legs?
Nickels and dimes man.
But the guys, they still like me.
And you know why?
'Cause I know how for *cook*!

The
Bath

We bathe after all the men.
Women dirty water.
My mother and I walk the long path
on the side of the anthurium grove
to the bathhouse.
Steamy and smoky,
the last embers of firewood
are dying in the copper burner
below the ofuro.

We undress.
Running her fingers
lightly through, she tests the water.
And so what if it burns,
she's a master of endurance.
Pailsful of scalding water are scooped up
and splashed over her body.

Lathering the towels with Ivory soap,
resting our feet on a duckboard,
we sit on a wooden bench,
our thighs touching.

She turns her back.
I scrub the line of her bones,
the line of small burn scars—
the yaito of her father's punishment.
"Harder, harder," she says,
her skin becoming red and shiny.
Moxa wafers and incense fire.
We rinse, climb into the tub
and slowly immerse ourselves.
Water claims our breasts.
It reaches our chins, and we soak,
blood rising to our temples.

The reflection of the bulb
bursts everytime I splash.
Soon, she starts telling me the story, again,
about the tsunami
that destroyed our house.
But I'm not in the mood for listening.
Unlike her, I'm not going
to have to brave men and water;
nothing can *ever* happen to me.

I catch air in my towel and float it:
here's an octopus, a jellyfish, a womb.
To muffle her voice,
I take a deep breath
and sink beneath water.

The
Waters
of
My
Body

Two days after giving birth,
my body was like a boat that sprung a leak—
breasts heavy with milk.
I wet the sheets.
I leaked through sleep and dreams.
I'd get up and my hair would be sticky,
matted like a cat's wet fur.
Milk gushed into the mouth
of my child, and sometimes,
I thought he'd choke
on all the milk my body made.
And who was I?
Young girl in a pony tail
too young to be a mother
who went out for walks
and grew spots on her t-shirts
that spread larger
than the high beams of passing cars.

I remember a young man,
both of us surprised
at sap rising, slowly,

like thermometer mercury,
the weight of semen.
And all summer,
in the back seat of his car,
the water of our bodies rose and fell—
a water table of desire
that entered into the pleasure
of our first experience.

The encounter with water
had always been met with surprise:
menarche, broken water bags, water in the lungs.
Each water with its own color,
its own peculiar smell.
Sweet or swampish,
or fishy,
like the open-air, seafood markets around town.
All my life
I could have drowned.

How is it that
the water has receded
from the shoreline of the body,
now that I'm older.
How is it that
all the water has abandoned
the sand, pebbles, driftwood,
left them open to the wind
and stranded above the waterline.

After
Smoke

Some of our greatest desires
we leave unindulged in the name of health:
salt, monosodium glutamate, sugar, cigarettes.
I smoked for the longest time.
It was a nasty habit,
but I loved every minute of it—
the smell, its look.

It was Grandfather smoking a pipe
as he worked;
or his hand-rolled Bull Durham
lit in an ebony holder,
the string bag pulled with teeth,
tobacco shreds poured from the pouch
on cigarette paper
like the laying of seed cane in the fields.
And me, trailing with an open mouth,
gulping the air like a fish.

It was those old
and bent women with black teeth

who came to visit,
the smoke and ashes dipping
in time to their sleep-nodding heads,
the comfortable talk and food.
They smoked as if sipping tea,
fingers stained and yellow.

It was the first loss of innocence.
A prelude to sex,
the neighbor girl's and mine,
when we almost burned
down the Taniguchi's garage
where we hid to light up
rolled newspaper cigarettes.
We emerged
with our eyebrows and ponytails singed,
all because Mr. Kadota, the storekeeper,
knew us well
and threatened to tell our mothers;
he refused to sell us
the cellophane-wrapped packets
we cast covetous eyes on
like boys we would lust after in later years.

Growing up, it was I,
playing make-believe—
thin and glamorous
in gowns of lamé
and surrounded by men;
blowing smoke into the air,
long-handled cigarette holders
dripping from an upturned hand

and slack fingers of cherry-red polished nails.
"Dah-ling," I cooed.

The romance of it all,
that's what I miss—
the long drag
after a meal, a drink,
or making love
that made a man stay, talk awhile.

Not Thinking of You

For Clarence Imada

1.

I cross the canal on Piopio Street.
I steal past the Boys Club
and go to Hilo Theater on the other
side of the street where
I join a line for tickets I don't buy.
This is a fifth-grader's ruse.
I go there to watch
the boys flit in and out
the barn doors of the club,
my real interest in acquiring
an acrylic heart pendant,
the boys' summer project.

The blue heart pendant you made
at the club is thick, a rock.
It swings like a pocket watch.
"I worked hard to make it," you apologize.
I never wear it. It is not
the same as a thin ruby lozenge
made by someone else
and flashing in a girlfriend's palm.

2.

Together, we steal past the offertory box,
go through the columbarium
where ashes in cardboard boxes
drizzle their contents
like termite droppings on the floor.
Sliding our backs on the wall,
we toe past the piles,
climb the steep staircase
and wind our way up to the bell tower.
Below us, we can hear the young adult Sunday service.
The Sanskrit chant rises like water
and washes over us,
our irreverence.
We laugh and mimic with our mouths:
        Buddham Saranam Gacchami
        Dhamman Saranam Gacchami
        Sangham Saranam Gacchami
Once at the top, you take my hand.
We sit, look over the whole city
as if it were ours to have.
Landmarks you point out: Hoʻolulu Park,
the Japanese tea garden, Coconut Island.
"Oh, it's so beautiful," I say,
already planning
to show the view to someone else.

3.

Silver-foiled paper umbrellas strung
with crepe-paper flowers hang upside
down from the high school gym ceiling.
This is the sky we dance under,

music by the Staffaires.
Umbrellas twirl their foiled facets
and catch the fluorescent light like diamonds.
We are two dateless friends.
You play along that this is a date of convenience.
You can't say what you want to say,
so you scan the dance floor over my shoulders.
You drop your head from one side to the other
like a wilted flower.
We hardly talk.

4.
Two weeks later,
you drown. You're found in mud.
Our classmates are your pallbearers.
We consecrate your body in a chant,
and we give you up:
one year, ten years, a hundred thousand years.
Baby-blue, satin lining tufts your coffin,
and we file past your open casket for one last look,
your lips purple, hands bluish
and clasped around an envelope,
a mortuary tablet and some prayer beads.
On your white suit,
a burgundy boutonniere like one I gave you.

The bonsan taps a mallet on the skull of the drum
as people go up to view your body.
Your family greets the line. My turn.
Your stepmother grasps my hands tightly.
She shakes them up and down
and cries into them.

But this does nothing to make up
for the thought that when we last danced,
my heart was not in it.
How careless I'd been of you.

Homeless

My son lives on the streets.
We don't see each other much.
Like a mother who puts white lilies
on the headstone of a dead child,
I put money into his bank account,
clothes into E-Z Access storage
and pretend he's far away—
at a boarding school, or in a foreign country.
Nights, I dream fairy tales about him.
I dream he becomes a prince,
scholar or warrior who rescues me
from sorrow, the way he rescued me
when he was a child and said,
"Mommy, don't cry," and brought tea
into the room of his father's acrimony—
brave, standing tall in the forest
fire of his father's scorn. I wake
to the empty sound of wind in the trees.
He says he wants to live with me.
I say I can't live with him—
boy whose words crash like branches in a rain storm.
Nothing can hold him in,

the walls of a house too thin.
Back home, I had seen
the "study-hard-so-you-don't-become-like-them"
street bums on Mamo Street,
and he's like *them*.
These days, in order to catch a glimpse of him,
I circle the city. One day,
I see him on his bike.
People give him wide berth,
the same way birds avoid power lines,
oncoming cars or trees.
I park on a side street.
Wild-eyed, he flies the block
as if in a holding pattern.
Not of my body, not of my hopes,
he homes in on what can't be given or taken away.

Feral

1. Kamanaiki Trail—1974

Pushing aside
the warm grasses
that bend into the narrow trail,
we move deep
into Kalihi Valley.
Our walk is suddenly
interrupted by what
the parted brush
reveals to us in the sun—
a feral dog and her pup;
our wild, lost, secret selves.

We back away
till we no longer see them.

2. Kāne'ohe State Hospital—1987

I drive on Likelike Highway
over the Pali.
I nose around therapy and prescription charts
at the hospital, looking for signs—
your getting better.

Son who hangs
on the teat of reality,
yours is not mine.
You speak of being
wired to brain scans,
of spirits talking about you.
I spin, chase tail,
find no one around. I hold on
to what is old and tangible instead—
juzu beads in my jacket pocket,
a Shinto omamori for your neck
to bite the leg
of this unknown evil.

3. Pali Ward, Patio Lockup

In the warmth
of this lockup,
you whimper,
bare your teeth,
sneer at me.
Runt of the litter,
some animals kill and eat,
I regret you
in the back of my fears.
I feel so pregnant
with desperation
as I watch you curl
like a blind pup.
Unresolved fetus
in this hospital wing.

Sadness paces all around us.
Nothing helps.
I appeal
in last resort,
to the ancient dictums
of our people:
oyakōkō, giri, on.
Even these entreaties
can't put you back together, again.
Old rules of behavior
betray us.
The rules don't help me,
and they mean nothing to you
in your paranoia.

Son,
After
the
Attempt

The sun dusts the nape of my neck, hotly.
Behind us, the deep-pleated Ko'olau rise.
I perspire. But you're cold in heavy
robes, sandals slapping as you pace. Our eyes
meet where I sit on a bench. You turn, size
me up, then point like some wild prophet and ask:
"Grandma Lee has Alzheimer's. When she dies,
will she be as she was, before the mask?
The paraplegic, will he be able
to walk, to pick flowers again? You do
know what it means to be alive—*stable*.
When we die, we die perfect, don't we?"
You take silence as assent. "Mom, so tell me
why do you and your miserable gods stop me?"

Encouragement

A day of encouragement!
You shuffle toward me
in your bright green and red
hospital gown, special for *bolters*,
your face, morning-moon-pale,
your eyes, sea-calm.

Drugged, you say it's like pulling water,
limp and heavy,
your days the stillness of ocean pools.
Once more a sleepy, thumb-sucking child,
hanging onto the arm of my voice
to be saved.

You ask for some Snickers,
sushi and heavy metal rock magazines.
Tears start falling.
They leap off a half-smile
like fish into the ache of my heart.
You get up. Walk away.

How lonely you look—

wrapped around the watery voices
you hear in your head.

The
First
Time

The hospital calls again.
You are brought in by ambulance
after you are discovered,
flopping like a fish on the sidewalk.

Every time is the first time.
I will never get used to it—
the late night calls,
the anxieties rising like tide,
the voices sounding far and fluid,
the nurses telling me
you are alive
but under observation.

But the worst time
was the first time—
the time when you took a fistful of sleeping pills,
and the nurse gave you some Ipecac
and fastened your slippery life
over the toilet bowl,
while I patted your back
in life's violent return.

Remember how the light and faces
wavered around us
detached as the moon
as if we were looking at things
from under water? To keep you awake,
I put my arms across your shoulders
like a receiving blanket
for the long walk ahead of us.
We dropped our heads, then,
to resist death,
slow-circling the room.

Bird

Feathers. My son was covered with feathers.
Everywhere. Head to toe.
Hair, ears, lashes, brows, clothes.
Thin as a quill, light as down,
he looked more like a bird
than anything human
when he materialized,
ruffled and nervous,
at the door of the hospital.

Lured by the flight of himself
to where birds by instinct survive,
he pushed himself into a crawl space,
a rafter in the city,
to lay down and die
among the roosting spotted doves
and city's pigeons.
All he could hear
were the avian whoop and throated
whir of the nesting birds.

At the last moment,
what impressed a plume of hope,
the desire to live,
to pick himself up
and walk into an emergency room?
Before this, where did his cries go?
And how was a mother to hear,
to know?—bird around my neck,
son who flew out of my hands—
in the distance of his agony and mine
not shortened by faith or love
or the stepping of the birds across his chest
between his arms and legs,
in a song and dance,
the scattering of crumbs, twigs and leavings.

Royally
Pissed

"*Talk* to him. He's still here.
I know these things," pronounces the nurse
in a dispensation of her experience,
years of watching the dying die.
"The soul hangs around for awhile."
But what can I say to you—
that I'm royally pissed,
that I'm madder than hell at you
God damn kid
how dare you do the right things at the end
and that it all came too late?
I want to slap you back to life,
scream and beat the drum
of your chest with my fists,
howl in the strange, hollow
animal cry of the crazed dog
that bays at the moon
behind the old mountain house,
then cuts loose across the fields
and stream, fanning water high in its wake,
the droplets caught in the moonlight
and flung into a hive of stars.

Forgive my crown of anger.
Deliver me from this fucking pain.

Late

For Darius

Skinny brother
leans his treeform
in the doorway
of your hospital room,
the smell of the flowers
too white and sweet
for what branches into his fears.
It's two in the morning.
His night aches for sleep,
but he can't put you
to rest, his mind
pressed into the days
we wait for you to die.
Stick arms and leg shadows
across your body.
"How he doing—okay?" he asks.

All his life
your brother's worried about you.
He still worries.
From when you were a young kid,
he's been tied to your wrist of hurt,

picking you up from the hospitals,
driving you home.
How your impatience
whacked him hard, in the gut—
Hurry up!—every time he was late.
But he'd do it over again,
in a minute.
He'd go out and break his back for you,
far better to have you alive,
give *anything*
to hear you say once more,
"Eh, where you was?"

Nest

I tighten the scarf around my neck,
grip my black coat
to resist the night's crazy wind,
the agonized air,
the whip of the branches.
Piling pillows and blankets around me,
I build a nest on a rollaway
next to your bed.
Feeding tubes and IV lines offer a covering.
Carrying its supply of air,
its smoke rings of oxygen,
your ventilator chugs,
uphill, like a train
into the broken wings of your lungs,
and departs
with your memory of what it is to be alive.
Live.   Live.

I agree. Pull the plug.
What does this have to do with the heart?
Now, it's just a matter of time—
a weed in a sidewalk crack,
a gold guitar.
Tonight, hovering over you,

I'm a new mother.
I listen to you breathe—
the same way I listened
when you were a child,
and I couldn't sleep
in the fear of such a miracle.
My ears to your life.
I watch for the slightest change,
each breath's soft and shallow retreat.
And your life goes scattering.
Son who leaned too far out of the window,
kicked shoes on the porch,
you who wanted more than just a breath of fresh air.
You thought you could fly.

Good
as
Gold

I bring your hands together,
weave your fingers into a prayerful position
and wind the sandalwood rosary beads around your wrists
to bind them for the last rites of the pillow.
Guardians of your last hours,
your brother and I stand at your bedside
and drink the potion of earthly truth
that is poured into our disbelief.
We will never see you again.

The ceremonial chime rings
and the sound moves you beyond,
the music of the chant celestial,
an elixir of everlasting life,
that alchemy of gold struck three times,
for luck, the philospher's stone's shine,
bone, flesh, we give up
forever and ever.

The
Struggle

In this rotation,
the bones of night,
Melissa, angel of mercy, works the graveyard shift.
Drifts in her whites like wind-caught sails.
Which one will go next?
Everyone on this floor critical,
the dying beyond sleep, agony, or self-pity.
In her rounds she administers
to the anguish of the living.
She gives lozenges of comfort,
cotton pats of sympathy.
I can hear her.
"Are you comfortable?"
"May I get you something?"
"More coffee or tea?"
Next door, she sings with members
of the Samoan family
who come and go
with their ukuleles and guitars,
songs for a dying father
who sleeps on a strip of tapa
shaped like a canoe

that will spirit him away.
She comes at last to your room.
Burdened by composure and kindness,
she drops herself on my cot
and grieves for a son who is like you,
stretched out
taut as strings on a guitar,
light shiny on your forehead,
a moon cleft of fluorescence.
She tells me that children like ours
are orphans of life,
and maybe, things would be different
if we could only take them back,
again, into ourselves.
"To start all over," she says.
I nod. It is the dream
of mothers whose children
have died like this, before their time,
a wish that plays itself over and over
like a broken record,
spinning the drama of those left behind.

The Permission

My son is lying like a bridge
spanning himself from this life
into another.
We will take down the scaffolding
that breathes for him,
each breath a step closer
to where he will arrive.
Hands raised, the nurse snaps the latex gloves
over her hands and unplugs the ventilator.
His mouth falls open
and she takes the tubes and pulls
them out of his throat,
feeding tube from his nose,
IV from his arm.
She leaves the oxygen in for comfort,
the last suspension to his life.
His head rolls back on the pillow.
Slack from pain and tension, his eyes open
and tears roll down his face.
I hold his hand and wipe his forehead,
the things I couldn't do to love him.
You're almost there.

He breathes on his own.
It's pure reflex now.
His breathing will slow down
they tell me, then fade.
He goes on through the night,
into the next day.
It will be nice where you go.
I give him this permission of love—
to cross the bridge.
I tell him to enter Kaiwiki house.
He doesn't have to take his shoes off
or shake out his pockets,
filled with the summer he played in.

In
a
Rush

The day I wait for my son to die,
it's as if we are down at the harbor
watching the ships go by and the longshoremen
cart pallets of iceberg lettuce, bananas and mail across the
　　　wharf.
Our last time together, we're made whole again
as in that perfect moment,
mother and child,
child no one could have loved
or wanted, except me, his mother.
Son brought to me in a blue blanket,
face red and swollen as a wound,
the day I tied on his first booties.
We'd grown apart since then,
joined now in this pitiable end,
facing the ocean.

All day no change.
Pulse, respiration, same.
I leave to eat the meat dry as saltines,
change my sandals, wash my face.

And it is so like him
to die without me there at his bedside,
his death as impulsive as he had always been—
with no bells or clamor of the triangle—
as if he had suddenly seen a passing ship,
wasn't about to miss it,
got up and dove into the water to meet it,
going out the same way he had come,
in a rush, headlong,
pushing through water
without a clue, boarding pass, or blessing.

The
Way

White candles and chrysanthemums
are an offering of continuity.
I cradle your urn to be blessed by the priest
and carry your mortuary tablet like a flame to the altar.
The seven-day service, over ashes,
inters your remains at the temple.

Mother, this is the way I come back to you.

Shoku Sho, the priest explains your Buddhist name
and places the peace you never had into your spirit.
For the sake of the living, we will hold observances:
forty-nine days, a hundred days, one year.
That your forty-ninth day, the day of compassion,
the day your spirit is released from Earth's bond
falls on my birthday is a wonderful omen.

You face the east,
the morning sun, the rise of eternity.
Each day the priest will strike the gong in a blessing
when morning breaks over Nu'uanu,

and you will hear the song of each day's naming.
I place pictures of happier times inside the niche.
You on your bike, riding into the valley,
eating oysters at Sydney's house,
feeding the deer at Kamakura.

This is the way, mother, I come back to you.

Country
of
Grief

After my son dies,
the earnestness of grief
makes me pack up my things to move to a new
blue country where time ticks its blue hours.
Everywhere I look, the blue mountains,
blue flowers, blue stars. Even the bells
toll a sad blue sound and ring
a chill that ices my breath and mouth.
The country of grief is beautiful
with its random towns and windswept chimney
stacks of blue smoke and shuttered houses,
the votive candles floating beyond
the indigo glare of curtains on windows,
the people behind them looking out,
offering no relief from sadness in the meadows,
the stones of forlorn sheep on the rolling hills—
a countryside of bottomless wells,
blue stalks of hyacinth,
and tall, stark silos,
holding the wheat of my sleep.

What
You
Say

In this room,
aqueous,
we stir slowly.
The low light is kind,
our arms heavy with care.

"I would have mourned you all my life
had you not been saved from water,
had you not lived,
and I would have missed you,
terribly, without really knowing why.
I would have searched faces of people
who dropped by the factory
or while I sorted yards of damask covering
or supervised the men,
working the garnett machines."

And you kiss me as you say this—
across my back,
over my ears, my lips.

It is good this way,

growing old with you,
our movements
straying into the shadows.
Later, I will slip
into something practical—
a flower-printed flannel nightgown.
And we will read in bed,
a bowl of fruit
and buttered crackers between us
that I will crunch and scatter—
bits on the sheets you'll not mind.
But for now,
consider only the body.
Awkward,
but tempered and fluid in this light—
graceful swimmers,
we move,
we move like waves.

Painter

Light
from the window
light
failing in her eyes,
my mother
a brush painter
drops her head closer to the paper
and follows the lines
each brush stroke
the road to a map
the sweep to where they lead.

It comes as a fluttering
almost a dull ache in the stomach.
She tells me
she feels this need
to hurry
paint as much as she can.
The press
of time a weight of white birds in her hands.

A scattering

everyday

like wildflowers on the roadside

and she steps out the doorway

to gather

the light before its shutting.

Through the pine trees

her hands pull

the last melon slice of moon she can see

clouds and branches

slow curves

of the long blades of grass

into what she loves to do most.

"How can I live," she asks, "when I go blind?"

At her desk

by noon

working till light thins like skin

I watch her

over the paper

close track of eyes

each brush stroke

a lucky charm, pressed clover, or shiny coin

to take with her on the road

to where she doesn't want to be found.

And she's happiest there

beyond the fences

her last hours playing

in a white and open field.

Acknowledgments

Grateful acknowledgment is made to the following publications in which some of these poems first appeared in slightly different forms: *Articulations: Poetry About Illness and the Body* ("Caregiver"); *Asian America Journal:* ("Son, After the Attempt"); *Bamboo Ridge, The Hawai'i Writers' Quarterly:* ("Coral Chips," "The First Time," "Joji and the Iceman" [previously published as "The Iceman"], "A Scolding from My Father," "The Smell of the Sea," "Womanhood"); *Chaminade Literary Review:* ("The Peddler"); *Constructions and Confrontations: Changing Representations of Women and Feminism East and West:* ("After Near Drowning," "Name," "The Waters of My Body," "What My Mother Confided in a Moment of Sadness"); *Dissident Song: A Contemporary Asian American Anthology:* ("No-Place Children"); *Hawai'i Herald:* ("Late Praise," "My Mother's Sugar Loaves," "Not Thinking of You" [previously published as "Careless of You"], "Only Son," "School Boy from Up Mauka," "A Spin Around Town"); *Kaya Anthology of New Asian American Poetry:* ("Atsuko's Wedding Day" [previously published as "Life Perfect"], "Before Time"); *Literary Arts Hawai'i:* ("Feral"); *Makali'i:* ("After Smoke," "Encouragement," "Old Biddies"); *Maps of Desire, An Asian American Erotic Anthology:* ("Tongue"); *Mother of the Groom Anthology:* ("Bedtime," "Champing at the Bit," "The Scolding," "Shower," "Suspicious," "Two Queens"); *The Seattle Review:* ("The Bath," "Hāla'i Hill").

Many thanks to David Lee, Eric Chock, Lois-Ann Yamanaka, and my study groups.

Special thanks to Cathy Song for her love, friendship and wisdom.

About the Author

Juliet S. Kono was born and raised in Hilo, Hawai'i. She earned a B.A. and M.A. from the University of Hawai'i at Manoa, and currently teaches English Composition at Leeward Community College. Her first book of poems, *Hilo Rains*, was published by Bamboo Ridge Press in 1988. She was a winner of the Elliot Cades Award for Literature and the James Clavell Award for fiction in 1991. She lives in Honolulu.